Rock On!

Soil

Chris Oxlade

 raintree
a Capstone company — publishers for children

Raintree is an imprint of Capstone Global Library Limited, a company incorporated in England and Wales having its registered office at 264 Banbury Road, Oxford, OX2 7DY – Registered company number: 6695582

www.raintree.co.uk
myorders@raintree.co.uk

Edited by Helen Cox Cannons
Designed by Philippa Jenkins
Illustrated by Stefan Chabluk p7, and Gary Jones p18
Original illustrations © Capstone Global Library Limited 2016
Picture research by Tracy Cummins
Production by Victoria Fitzgerald
Originated by Capstone Global Library Limited
Printed and bound in China

ISBN 978 1 474 7 1407 5
19 18 17 16 15
10 9 8 7 6 5 4 3 2 1

British Library Cataloguing in Publication Data
A full catalogue record for this book is available from the British Library.

Acknowledgements
We would like to thank the following for permission to reproduce photographs: Alamy: Dorling Kindersley ltd, 16; Capstone Press: Gary Jones, 18, Stefan Chabluk, 7, Karon Dubke, 28, 29; Getty Images: Eco Images, 27; NOAA: George E. Marsh Album, 22; Science Source: Alexandre Petzold, 8, David Scharf, 19, Michael P. Gadomski, 13, Michael Szoenyi, 12, Pascal Goetgheluck, 21; Shutterstock: B Brown, 4, bogdanhoda, 24, Dirk Ercken, 26, Grimplet, 17, Madlen, 10, Matt Gibson, 9, Pawel Kazmierczak, 6, schankz, Cover, 1, The Visual Explorer, 25; SuperStock: Cultura Limited, 11; Thinkstock: nameinfame, 14, Rainer Kühnl, 23, Tatiana Grozetskaya, 20

The author would like to thank Dr Gillian Fyfe for her invaluable help in the preparation of this book.

Contents

Some words are shown in bold, **like this**. You can find out what they mean by looking in the glossary.

What is soil?

Soil is a natural material. It is a mixture of bits of rock, bits of rotting plants, living things, air and water. Wherever you live in the world, there will be some soil close by. Soil is in flowerbeds, in flowerpots, under lawns and sports pitches, in woods and anywhere there's mud. Soil is easy to see where farmers have just ploughed their fields.

This farmland soil is being prepared for growing crops.

Where we find soil

We find soil on the surface of Earth. In valleys and on plains it covers up the rocks that make up Earth's **crust**. There is no soil where there is bare rock, or on the two-thirds of Earth that is covered with oceans, seas and **ice sheets**.

Where soil comes from

The rocky bits in soil are made when rocks on the surface get broken into pieces by the weather, flowing water, wind and waves. The bits of rotting plants come from plants that grow in the soil.

Why soil is important

Soil is **vital** for plants. Plants put their roots into soil to support themselves. Also, plants get the water and **minerals** they need to grow and live from soil. We need soil to grow crops for food, to grow trees for wood and to grow flowers and other plants in gardens. Soil is also a **habitat** for animals and other living things, such as worms and insects.

ROCK SOLID FACTS!

FILLED WITH LIFE

The soil is full of living things. There are more **bacteria** in a handful of soil than there are people living on Earth!

What is soil like?

How would you describe the soil in your garden, local park or in a plant pot? It might be very dark grey, dark brown or reddish brown. Look a bit closer and you might be able to see what the soil is made of. You might see bits of rock, bits of rotting leaves and twigs and possibly some small animals crawling in it.

Soil colour

Some soils are very dark because they contain bits of dark-coloured rock or lots of rotting plants. Some soils are grey because they contain colourless bits of rock. Some soils are brown or reddish brown. This is because they are made of rocky bits that contain iron. <u>Soil always looks darker when it is wet, and lighter when it dries out.</u>

This red soil in the Canary Islands, Spain, is formed from volcanic rock.

This diagram shows the different layers in soil. ⟹

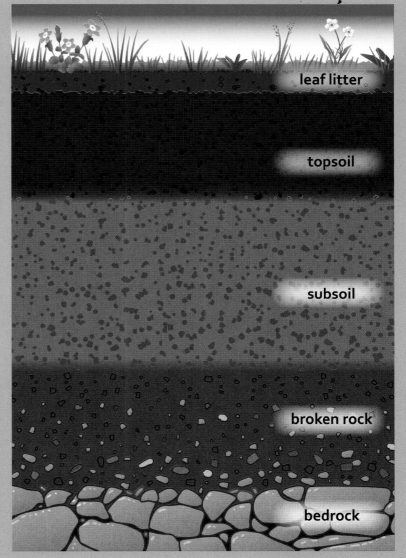

leaf litter

topsoil

subsoil

broken rock

bedrock

Soil texture

Texture is how the soil feels. If you scoop up a handful of soil and rub it between your fingers, it might feel smooth, or it might feel gritty and rough. You might find that it sticks together, or that it crumbles easily.

Layers of soil

The soil we see on the ground is the very top layer of soil, called **topsoil**. If you dig down into soil past the topsoil, you find another layer of soil that is a different colour or texture. This layer is called **subsoil**. If you kept digging down, you would eventually come to solid rock below the soil, called bedrock. Bedrock is the top layer of rock in Earth's **crust**.

In a handful of garden soil, a bit less than half is made up of small pieces of rock. Scientists call these small pieces **mineral particles**. <u>Minerals are the materials from which rocks are made.</u>

A small part of a handful of soil is made of rotting bits of plants, such as rotting leaves and twigs. The rest of the handful of soil is made up of air and water.

Rocky bits

The mineral particles in soil are very small and are made of sand, silt or clay. Sand particles are the largest. Silt particles are smaller than sand particles. Clay particles are even smaller than silt particles. In most soils, there is a mixture of particles of different sizes, and often there are pebbles and stones.

This soil contains large chunks of rock.

Leaf litter on the floor of a woodland.

Rotting material

The rotting bits found within soil are called **organic matter.** Organic matter is made up of rotting dead animals and bits of living plants, such as fallen leaves, seeds and fruits, rotting logs, branches and twigs.

In woodlands and forests, the soil is often hidden beneath a layer of dead leaves called leaf litter. Organic matter that has been rotting for a few months is called **humus**. It is dark in colour and well mixed up with the mineral particles.

ROCK SOLID FACTS!

SMELLY SOIL

If you sniff a handful of damp soil, you'll detect an "earthy" smell. The smell comes from **bacteria** that live in the soil. Some desert animals, such as rattlesnakes, use this smell to detect water to drink.

This soil has lots of gaps in it, filled with air.

Air, water and minerals

Imagine a jar filled with pebbles. In between the pebbles, there would be plenty of gaps filled with air. The same thing happens in soil – there are lots of tiny spaces between the **mineral particles** that are filled with air.

Water clings to these mineral particles and soaks into the **organic matter**. As a result, the minerals dissolve into the water. Air spaces disappear if the soil becomes **waterlogged**.

ROCK SOLID FACTS!

AIR SPACES

If you fill a bucket with soil from the garden, about a quarter of the bucket will be taken up by air pockets in the soil. Another quarter will be taken up by water.

We use sieves to separate soils into their parts.

Soil types

There are several different types of soil. Each soil contains a different mixture of mineral particles and organic matter. Here are the main types:

Sand	This soil is light brown in colour, and is rough and gritty. Water drains through this soil well.
Clay	This soil is reddish brown in colour, and it feels very smooth and sticky. The soil does not drain well, but minerals cling to the particles, so it can be a good soil for growing crops.
Silt	This soil is dark, and feels soft and smooth. It is dumped by rivers on the land along river banks.
Chalk	This soil is very light in colour, and feels gritty. It often contains larger bits of rock.
Peat	This soil is very dark brown, and feels spongy and damp. It contains lots of organic matter and **humus**.
Loam	This soil is a mixture of other soils. It is the sort of soil found in many gardens.

How is soil made?

We know that soil is made from bits of rock and bits of rotting plants. Think about the soil in your garden. The rocky bits were made when rocks were broken up and carried to your garden. The rocks they came from are called **parent material**. Two natural processes, called **weathering** and **erosion**, broke up the rocks. The **organic matter** in soil comes from plants and animals that grow and live in the soil.

Weathering breaks up rocks

Weathering happens when the weather, and sometimes plants, break up rocks into smaller pieces, such as scree. Weathering is a very slow process. It takes about 200–400 years for the weather, ice and plants to break up enough rock to make a layer of soil just 1 centimetre (0.4 inch) deep.

Scree is broken rock made by weathering.

The roots of this tree have pushed into a crack, breaking up a boulder.

Weathering breaks up rock in three ways:

Physical weathering	On hot days, rocks are heated up during the day, and cool down at night. The rock expands (gets bigger) when it gets hotter, and contracts (gets smaller) when it cools down. This weakens the rock, and bits fall off. Rocks are also broken up by ice. When the water in a crack in rock freezes, the ice pushes against the rock, making the crack bigger. In the end, the rock breaks in two.
Chemical weathering	When rain seeps into rock, it can slowly dissolve some of the **minerals** in the rock. Then the **particles** of rock fall apart.
Biological weathering	The roots of trees and other plants often push their way into cracks in rock. This widens the crack and can break rocks apart. **Algae** that grow on the surface of rocks also break up the rocks.

Erosion moves rocks

Erosion happens when natural forces move bits of loose rock. The natural forces are gravity, flowing water, wind, waves on the shore and ice in glaciers.

The beach is a good place to see erosion at work. A stream flowing across the sand picks up sand and moves it downwards. The wind picks up dry sand and moves it along the beach. Waves move sand up, down and along the beach.

Weathering and erosion have produced soil for a plant to grow in an unlikely place.

Glaciers

A glacier is a slow-moving river of ice. Glaciers and **ice sheets** cause erosion by scraping away at rocks and causing loose bits to move.

Dumping sediment

All the tiny pieces of rock that are moved by erosion get dumped somewhere. For example, pieces of rock that are washed down a river often get dumped next to the river during floods. They make a layer of rock **particles** that is ready to be turned into new soil.

Sources of organic matter

Tiny **organisms,** such as **algae** and **lichens,** start growing on new rock particles. Seeds blown by the wind land and germinate (start growing into new plants). When these plants die, animals such as worms arrive to feed on the **organic matter**. The worms mix the organic matter with the rock particles. And so slowly a layer of new soil is formed.

What lives in soil?

Soil is a **habitat** for animals, plants and other **organisms**. All these animals, plants and living things do important jobs in keeping soil in good condition. You may have seen earthworms squirming through soil and rabbit holes on hillsides. But most living things in soil are too small to see.

Earthworms in soil

Earthworms are pink worms that grow to about 8 centimetres (3 inches) in length. They burrow through the soil, eating the soil and digesting **organic matter**.

Earthworms mix up the organic materials and rocky **particles** and leave tunnels behind them. This helps to spread **nutrients** through the soil, and lets air and water into the soil.

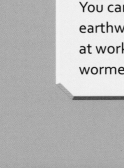

You can see earthworms at work in a wormery.

HOW MANY EARTHWORMS ARE IN SOIL?

There are lots of earthworms in the healthy soil of a meadow. There could be 100 worms in 1 square metre (11 square feet) of soil. That would mean around 1 million worms in an area the size of a football pitch!

Nematodes and other insects in soil

Nematodes are animals such as tiny worms that live in the soil. They are less than 2 millimetres (0.08 inches) long. There are many types of insects, centipedes and mites in the soil, too. All these animals feed on plant material and other organisms in the soil.

Burrowing animals in soil

Some small animals make their homes by burrowing into soil. They include rabbits, moles and badgers. The soil gives them shelter from the weather and from predators. The soil also insulates them (protects them from the cold) at night and in winter.

Moles burrow into the soil for safety and to find food.

Plants in soil

Plant roots grow down into the soil. The roots support the parts of the plants that are above the ground, stopping the plants from toppling over. Roots also collect the water and **nutrients** that the plant needs from the soil.

Roots

Small plants have short roots that grow down into the soil. Trees have much longer roots. If you see a fallen tree with its roots pulled up, you can see that tree roots grow down and sideways through the soil in every direction. There are also plant seeds and bulbs in the soil. Bulbs are like food stores for plants whose stems and leaves die away in winter.

This bacteria from soil has been magnified 27,000 times.

Soil recyclers

Like animals, plants help to keep soil healthy. When plants die, their nutrients go back into the soil. Then **organisms** in the soil feed on the dead plants. Plant roots help to bind the soil together. Without them, dry soil can be blown away.

Micro-organisms are animals, plants and other organisms in the soil that are too small to see unless we look at them through a microscope. Micro-organisms include **bacteria, algae** and fungi. They feed on **organic matter**, making it rot away. This releases the **minerals** in the matter into the soil. So micro-organisms also help to recycle nutrients from dead plants so that new plants can use them to grow.

ROCK SOLID FACTS!

FULL OF LIFE

A teaspoon of soil from a garden may contain 10,000 different sorts of bacteria and fungi!

Growing food is the most important use of soil. We need to grow enough food to feed all the people and farm animals on Earth. Farmers grow crops in the soil in their fields for everyone, while gardeners grow crops in their gardens to feed themselves or their families. Farmers and gardeners make sure that their plants get enough **nutrients** to grow.

Fertile soil

<u>**Fertile** soil is soil in which plants can grow well. A fertile soil is rich in nutrients.</u> In woodland, in a rainforest or in a meadow, plants take up the **minerals** from the soil that they need to help them grow. When the plants die or their leaves fall to the ground, the **organisms** in the soil help rot them down, and the nutrients are returned to the soil. So the soil stays fertile.

Volcanic soil is very fertile, such as this soil in Bali.

Putting minerals back

Few dead plants or leaves fall onto farm soil, because farmers harvest the crops in their fields every year. So the crops use up minerals in the soil but the nutrients are not returned to the soil. Farmers have to replace nutrients to keep the soil healthy. To do this, they put **organic matter**, such as manure, straw, rotting leaves and **compost** onto the soil, or use man-made **fertilizers**. Gardeners keep their soil healthy by using compost and plant food in their gardens.

ROCK SOLID FACTS!

CROPS IN THE DESERT

The River Nile in Egypt flows through desert. But it has a strip of fertile land along each side, where farmers can grow crops. This is because when the river floods it drops lots of fresh mineral **particles** on the land.

Improving soils

The best soils for growing crops and other plants contain plenty of **minerals**. They also contain just the right amount of water. Some soils are not so good. If they don't contain enough minerals, plants cannot grow properly. If they contain too much water because of poor drainage, air is forced out and plant roots die.

ROCK SOLID FACTS!

THE DUST BOWL

In the 1920s, farmers in the US and Canada ploughed up the grassy soil on the huge flat plains so they could plant crops. But during the 1930s, hardly any rain fell. Crops could not grow and the soil dried out. Because the grass had been removed, there was nothing to hold the soil together, and the soil blew away.

Gardeners add **compost** to their soil for growing vegetables and fruits.

Draining water

If water drains away too fast, soil gets too dry and can blow away. Farmers can improve poor soils. Mixing straw and manure into soil adds organic matter and minerals. This helps dry soil to keep hold of water.

Choosing plants

Different plants grow well in different types of soil. For example, cabbages grow well in clay soil, but not so well in sandy soils. Carrots grow well in sandy soils, but not so well in clay soils. Gardeners have to choose the right plants for the soils they have in their gardens.

Ploughing

Farmers plough their fields after harvesting crops. Ploughing turns over the top layer of soil. This helps to bury any rotting plant material, brings fresh soil to the surface and loosens the soil. It gets the soil ready for farmers to sow seeds for new crops.

The main way we use soil is for growing crops and other plants. But soil has other uses, too. Engineers use soil when they are building roads and dams, potters use clay soil to make pottery and gardeners use some soils as **compost**.

Building with soil

Engineers pile soil into heaps to make embankments for roads and railways. They have special soil-moving machines that scrape, dig, spread out and roll soil. Engineers also use soil to build enormous dams, called earth-filled dams, for holding back water to make reservoirs (lakes or ponds used to store water).

Dams often have a layer of clay inside to stop water seeping through. Soil banks called levees are built along riverbanks. Levees stop land beside a river from getting flooded when the river is very full after heavy rain.

This bulldozer is moving soil to where it's needed on a construction site.

Mud brick walls in the Sahara Desert.

Pots and bricks

Clay sticks together in clumps when it is damp. Potters mould damp clay into pots and other containers. Then they heat the clay in an oven called a kiln, which makes the clay go hard, like rock. In dry, hot places, bricks are made from clay soil mixed with straw, then dried in the hot sunshine.

Peat for compost and fuel

Peat soil is full of **organic matter**, so it contains lots of **minerals**. That's why peat is often used as compost for planting pot plants, and for making other soils more **fertile**. Peat is also used as a fuel, because dried peat burns well.

ROCK SOLID FACTS!

HISTORY IN THE SOIL

Soil often contains objects such as bits of crockery, buttons and coins that were lost hundreds of years ago. These objects tell **archaeologists** how people lived in the past. Archaeologists are people who study ancient remains of people, their buildings and belongings.

25

Why should we look after soil?

We've seen how important soil is for growing crops. Soil is important for humans and animals, as well as plants in the wild. Without plants growing in soil, animals would have nothing to eat and many would have no **habitats** to live in.

Eroding delicate soils

Rainforest soils are especially delicate. Thousands of rainforest trees are cut down every day for their timber. The forest is cleared and dirt roads are built for trucks to carry the timber away. The plant roots that hold the soil together die and the soil becomes loose.

When rain falls, it washes the soil away into streams and rivers. Farmers also damage rainforest soil by cutting down the forest to make space for crops. After a few years the soil runs out of **nutrients**. The farmers move away, but often the soil cannot recover.

Soil has been washed away here because trees have been cut down.

New trees are being planted in Peru to stop soil **erosion**. ⬅

Creating floods

Soil helps to stop floods. When it rains, the soil in fields and forests soaks up the water and releases it slowly. Where soil has been washed away or replaced by roads or paths, rain runs straight off into streams and rivers. This can cause the streams and rivers to flood.

Soil for the planet

We have seen that soil is **vital** for plants and animals to survive, but soil is easy to damage. If we don't take care of soil, it can be lost forever. We need to look after soil for the good of our planet.

ROCK SOLID FACTS!

GLOBAL WARMING

You may have heard of a problem called global warming. Experts think that a gas called carbon dioxide, which is made when we burn fuels, is slowly heating up our planet. Soils are helping to fight global warming because they soak up about 10 per cent of the carbon dioxide we make.

You can find out what's in soil by looking at the soil close-up with a magnifying glass. Start by looking at some soil you have found from your garden, a plant pot, a field or your local park. Try to get samples of soils from different places. Then compare what's in the different soils by separating it into: different **mineral particles**, stones, **organic matter** and living things.

What you need:

- soil
- an old tray
- a small magnifying glass (called a hand lens)
- a large, clean jar with a lid
- some water

1 Collect a handful of soil. Spread the soil out on an old tray and look at it closely with a magnifying glass. Can you:
- see bits of rocks?
- see bits of rotting plants?
- see any worms or minibeasts?

2 Take another handful of soil and put it into a large glass jar. Fill the jar about three-quarters full with water. Put the lid tightly on and shake the jar to mix the water and soil.

28

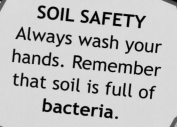

SOIL SAFETY
Always wash your hands. Remember that soil is full of **bacteria**.

❸ Put the jar in a place where it won't be disturbed and leave it for a few hours.

❹ Look carefully at the layers of material in the jar. You should see some organic matter floating on top of the water. There will be rock particles at the bottom of the jar. There will probably be layers of particles, with the largest **particles** at the bottom and the smallest particles at the top. You might see some tiny animals in the water.

❺ If you leave the jar for a few more hours, the tiny particles that made the water look muddy will settle to the bottom, too.

Glossary

algae tiny, plant-like living thing

archaeologist scientist who studies how people lived in the past

bacteria tiny living things that can only be seen through a microscope

compost mixture of decaying plant matter put into soil to fertilize it

crust thin layer of hard rock that makes up the surface of Earth

erosion wearing away of the landscape by flowing water, wind, waves and ice

fertile full of the nutrients that plants need to grow well

fertilizer substance used to make crops grow better

habitat place where an animal or plant lives

humus dark-coloured, rotting plant material that is part of soil

ice sheet sheet of ice hundreds of metres thick that lies on top of a mountain range

lichen simple plant that grows on rocks and trees and looks like moss

minerals natural, non-living materials found in Earth's crust

nutrients chemicals in the soil that plants need to grow and live

organic matter dead and rotting parts of animals and plants that are in the soil

organism any living thing, animal or plant

parent material rock that is broken up to make the mineral particles in soil

particle tiny piece of matter only seen using a microscope

subsoil layer of soil under the topsoil

topsoil top layer of soil, containing organic matter

vital of life and death importance

waterlog fill with water

weathering breaking up of rocks by the actions of either the weather, chemicals or plants

Books

Experiments with Soil (My Science Investigations), Christine Taylor-Butler (Heinemann Library, 2011)

Soil Basics (Science Builders), Mari C. Shuh (Capstone Press, 2011)

Why Do We Need Soil? (Natural Resources Close-Up) Kelley MacAulay (Crabtree, 2014)

Websites

http://www.bbc.co.uk/education/clips/z7rb4wx
In this BBC Bitesize video, a scientist explains what soil is and what it is made from.

http://www.bbc.co.uk/bitesize/ks2/science/materials/ rocks_soils/play/
This fun BBC *Sarah Jane Adventures* game will test your knowledge on rocks and soils.

http://www.soil-net.com/primary
This website has fun interactive information about soils.

Index